FRENCH SLANGUAGE

A FUN VISUAL GUIDE TO FRENCH TERMS AND PHRASES BY MIKE ELLIS

GIBBS
TO ENRICH AND INS

DEDICATED TO ALL THOSE WHO THOUGHT LEARNING FRENCH WAS DIFFICULT.

First Edition
21 20 19 18 17   16 15

Published by
Gibbs Smith
P.O. Box 667
Layton, Utah 84041

1.800.835.4993 orders
www.gibbs-smith.com

Designed by michelvrana.com
Printed and bound in Hong Kong
Gibbs Smith books are printed on paper produced
from sustainable PEFC-certified forest/controlled
wood source. Learn more at www.pefc.org.

Library of Congress Cataloging-in-Publication
Data

Ellis, Mike, 1961-
  French slanguage : a fun visual guide to French
terms and phrases / Mike Ellis. — 1st ed.
     p. cm.
  ISBN 978-1-4236-2244-4
1. French language—Conversation and phrase
books—English. I. Title.
  PC2121.E454 2012
  448.3'421—dc23
                          2011041613

CONTENTS

HOW TO USE THIS BOOK

If you have always wanted to learn the basics of French, but traditional methods seemed overwhelming or intimidating, this book is for you! Just follow the directions below and soon you'll be able to say dozens of words and phrases in French.

• Follow the illustrated prompts and say the phrase quickly and smoothly. Emphasize the word highlighted in red. In French, it is almost always the last word in the sentence or phrase. A strikethrough means don't pronounce that letter.

• There are no distinctions made in this book between masculine/feminine, singular/plural, formal/familiar, indirect object pronouns, intransitive verbs, etc.

• Learn to string together words or phrases to create many more phrases.

• Draw your own pictures to help with memorization and pronunciation.

Note: This book may produce Americanized French.

For free sound bytes, visit slanguage.com.

GREETINGS AND RESPONSES

Welcome *Bienvenu*	**Bee Evan Knew**
It's a pleasure *C'est une plaisir*	**Set Tune Plays Ear**
His name is . . . *Il s'appelle . . .*	**Eel Sop Pell . . .**
Her name is . . . *Elle s'appelle . . .*	**Elsa Pell . . .**

It's necessary . . .
Il faut que . . .

Eel Folk ...

Thank you very much
Merci beaucoup

Mare See Bow Coo

It's for you
C'est pour vous

Say Pour Voo

If it pleases you
S'il vous plaît

See Voo Play

Right?
N'est-ce pas?

Ness Pa?

Yes, yes
Oui, oui

We We

Sorry
Desolé

Daze Oh Lay

Nice gift
Beau cadeau

Bow Cod Doe

You're a fool
Tu es bête

2A Bet

Aim May

To like
Aimer

You like them?
Tu les aimes?

2 Lays Am?

You hate them?
Tu les détestes?

2 Lay Day Test?

Pretty baby
Beau bébé

Bow Bay Bay

Bun a Me

Good friend
Bon ami

Mother
Mère

Mare

Father
Père

Pear

Stepmother
Belle-mère

Bell Mare

Sister-in-law
Belle-soeur

Bell Sir

Beautiful niece
Belle nièce

Bell Knee Yes

Beautiful granddaughter
Belle petite fille

Bell Pet Tee Fee

Handsome boyfriend
Beau petit ami

Bow Pet Tia Me

Beautiful girlfriend
Bel petite amie

Bell Pet Teet Tom Me

Beautiful girl
Belle fille

Bell Fee

It's a crowd
C'est une foule

Set Tune Fool

Drank
Bu

Boo

Believed
Cru

Crew

Owed
Dû

Due

Said
Dit

Dee

Read
Lu

Lou

Known
Su

Sue

To let
Laisser

Lay Say

To dry
Sécher

Say Shay

To drop
Laisser tomber

Lay Say Tom Bay

To explain
Expliquer

Ex Plea Kay

To blow
Souffler

Sue Flay

To remember
Se souvenir

Sis Sue Ven Ear

To shake
Secouer

Say Sue Way

To steal
Voler

Voe Lay

To spend
Passer

Pa Say

To do
Faire

Fair

To sleep
Dormir

Dorm Ear

To smoke
Fumer

Foo May

To fold
Plier

Plea Yay

To read
Lire

Lear

To become
Devenir

Devon Ear

To fall
Tomber

Tom Bay

To go
Aller

Ah Lay

To slide
Glisser

Glee Say

ADJECTIVES AND ADVERBS

Are you disappointed?
Es-tu déçu?

A2 Day Sue?

We're crazy
Nous sommes fous

New Sum Foo

It's popular
C'est populaire

Say Pope Poo Lair

Are you anxious?
Es-tu inquiète?

A2 An Key Yet?

It's idiotic
C'est imbécile

Say Am Bay Seal

Dishonest
Malhonnête

Mallon Net

You're honest
Tu es honnête

2A Owe Net

Independent
Indépendant

An Day Pawn Dawn

He's handsome
Il est beau

Eel Lay Bow

She's beautiful
Elle est belle

L.A. Bell

Is it ugly?
Est-ce c'est laid?

Essay Lay?

Divorced
Divorcée

Dee Vore Say

Yes, it's calm
Oui, c'est calme

We Say Calm

Impatient
Impatient

Am Pa See Yawn

Well dressed
Bien habillé

Bee Anna Bee Yay

You're artistic
Tu as artistiques

2A Are Tee's Teak

That's odd
C'est bizarre

Say Bee's Are

That's stupid
C'est bête

Say Bet

You're likeable
Tu es sympathique

2A Sam Pot Teak

Good idea
C'est une bonne idée

Set Tune Bunny Day

Bad idea
C'est une mal idée

Set Tune Molly Day

Foolish idea
C'est une idée bête

Set 2 Knee Day Bet

No idea
Aucune idée

Oh Cooney Day

Yes, it's perfect
Oui, c'est parfait

We Say Par Fay

It's complete
C'est complet

Say Come Play

Yes, it's early
Oui, il est tôt

We Eel Lay Toe

It's a lot
C'est beaucoup

Say Bow Coo

Usually
D'habitude

Dabby 2'd

Always *Toujours*	**2 Shore**
Under *Sous*	**Sue**
Also *Aussi*	 **Oh See**
Immediately *Aussitôt*	 **Oh See Toe**

PRONOUNS, PREPOSITIONS, AND CONJUNCTIONS

He
Il

Eel

She
Elle

Ell

We
Nous

New

They
Ils

Eel

Who?
Qui?

Key?

All
Tout

2

Whose
À qui

Ah Key

But
Mais

May

FOOD AND RESTAURANTS

We like . . .
On aime . . .

On Am ...

We don't like . . .
On n'aime pas . . .

On Am Pa ...

Beer, please
La bière, s'il vous plait

Lobby Air See Voo Play

Some coffee
Du café

Due Café

Lemonade
La limonade

Lolly Moan Nod

Some water
De l'eau

D'Low

Some milk
Du lait

Due Lay

Some tea
Du thé

Due Tay

Bottle of water
Bouteille d'eau

Boo Tie Doe

The best
Les meilleurs

Lay May Yer

Knife
Couteau

Coat Toe

Some butter
Du beurre

Due Burr

Tomatoes
Des tomates

Day Toe Mutt

To have dinner
Diner

Dee Nay

Some chicken
Du poulet

Due Poo Lay

Melons
Les melons

Lay May Lawn

My noodles
Mes nouilles

May New We

Sausages
Les saucisses

Lay So Cease

Lamb chops
Côtelettes d'agneau

Coat Tell Let Don Yo

Frying pans
Les poêles

Lay Poe Well

Eight cabbages
Huit choux

Wheat Shoe

Some dessert?
Du dessert?

Due Days Air?

Who likes cake?
Qui aime les gâteaux?

Key Am Lay Got Toe?

Some chocolate
Du chocolat

Due Show Coal Ah

Are we finished?
On a fini?

On Ah Fee Knee?

Who pays?
Qui paie?

Key Pay?

Yum
Miam

Me Yum

Menu
Le menu

Lemon New

To the bank
À la banque

Allah Bonk

To the market
Au marché

Oh Mar Shea

To the supermarket
Au supermarché

Oh Sue Pay Mar Shea

How much does it cost?
C'est combien?

Say Come Bee Yen?

Yes, it's stylish
Oui, c'est chic

We Say Shiek

Yes, it's expensive
Oui, c'est cher

We Say Share

Some fabric
Du tissu

Due Tee Sue

My boots
Mes bottes

May Boat

Nice hat
Beau chapeau

Bow Shah Poe

My socks
Mes chaussettes

May Show Set

Nice suit
Beau complet

Bow Come Play

My sneakers
Mes baskets

May Bus Kay

Beautiful ring
Belle bague

Bell Bog

Eyeglasses
Des lunettes

Day Lou Net

That's a beautiful sport coat
C'est une belle veste

Set Tune Bell Vest

Nice bikini
Beau bikini

Bow Bee Key Knee

Soldiers
Les soldats

Lay Sole Dot

Lawyer
L'avocat

Love Oh Cot

Cook
La cuisinier

Lock We See Knee Air

My methods
Mes méthodes

May May Toad

It's complete
C'est complet

Say Come Play

Four kilograms
Quatre kilos

Cat Key Low

Yes, it's high
Oui, c'est haut

We Say Owe

To weigh
Peser

Pay Say

Yes, it's hot
Oui, c'est chaud

We Say Show

It's liquid
C'est liquide

Say Lee Key'd

It's soft
C'est doux

Say Due

Ladder
L'échelle

Lay Shell

Tool
L'outil

Lou Tee

Pumps
Les pompes

Lay Pump

Scissors
Les ciseaux

Lay See So

Pliers
Les tenailles

Lay 10 Eye

HEALTH AND MEDICINE

To cough
Tousser

2 Say

Runny nose
Nez qui coule

Neigh Key Cool

It's strong
C'est fort

Say 4

To the pharmacy
À la pharmacie

Allah Farm a See

Crutches
Les bequilles

Lay Bay Key

Good blood
Beau sang

Bow Song

Stethoscope
Stéthoscope

Stay Toe Scope

Backache
Mal au dos

Ma Low Doe

Shoulder
L'épaule

Lay Paul

Stomach
L'estomac

Lace Toe Mock

Our noses
Nos nez

No Neigh

Beautiful skin
Belle peau

Bell Poe

Armpit
L'aisselle

Lie Sell

Doctor
Medecin

Made Sang

Tired
Fatigue

Fat Tee Gay

Hotel
L'hôtel

Low Tell

To the castle
Au château

Oh Shah Toe

To the movies
Au cinéma

Oh See Name Ah

To the museum
Au musée

Oh Moo Say

To the swimming pool
À la piscine

Allah Pea Scene

To the platform
Au quai

Okay

To the taxi
Au taxi

Oh Tock See

To the Folies Bergère
Au Folies Bergère

Oh Foe Lee Bear Share

To the zoo
Au zoo

Oh Zoo

Motorcycles
Les motos

Lay Moe Toe

Some camels
Des chameaux

Day Shah Moe

Some seagulls
Des mouettes

Day Moo Wet

A thousand mosquitos
Mil moustique

Meal Moose Teak

Some bees
Des abeilles

Daze a Bay

My pretty cats
Mes beaux chats

May Bow Shah

Snails
Les escargots

Lays Ace Car Go

Cattle
Les bétail

Lay Bay Tie

Pretty puppies
Beaux chiots

Bow She Owe

Mammals
Les mammifères

Lay Mummy Fair

Tortoises
Les tortues

Lay Tore 2

Some butterflies
Des papillons

Day Poppy Yawn

Domestic
Domestique

Doe Mess Teak

One
Une

Un

Two
Deux

Duh

Three
Trois

Twa

Four
Quatre

Cat

Five
Cinq

Six
Six

Seven
Sept

Eight
Huit

Sank

Cease

Set

Wheat

Nine
Neuf

Nerf

Ten
Dix

Deece

Eleven
Onze

Oz

Twelve
Douze

Dues

Hundred
Cent

Sawn

Thousand
Mille

Meal

Million
Million

Me Yawn

It is noon
Il est midi

Eel Lay Mee Dee

Right away
Tout suite

Toot Sweet

Are we early?
Sommes-nous tôt?

Sum New Toe?

Five minutes
Cinq minutes

Sank Me Newt

That time
Cette époque

Set Tay Poke

It's fall
C'est l'automne

Say Low Tum

Is it summer?
Est-ce c'est l'été?

Essay Lay Tay?

It's wrong
C'est faux

Say Foe

To the high school
Au lycée

Oh Lee Say

Mistakes
Les faute

Lay Foe

Mathematics
Les mathematiques

Lay Ma Tame a Teak

Physics
La physique

La Fee Seek

Economics
L'économie

Lay Kono Me

My grades
Mes notes

May Note

Chemistry
Chimie

She Me

School *L'école*	**Lay Cole**
Words *Les mots*	**Lay Moe**
Good idea *Bonne idée*	**Bunny Day**
Lists *Les listes*	**Lay Least**

To whisper
Chuchoter

Shoe Show Tay

Poetry
Des poésies

Day Poe Way See

To the picnic
Àu pique-nique

Oh Peak Neak

What a poet!
Quel poète!

Kelp Poe Wet

Heads or tails?
Pile ou face

Pea Lou Fuss

To the movies
Au cinéma

Oh See Name Ah

Comedy
Comédie

Comb May Dee

Santa Claus
Père Noël

Pear No Well

Six flutes
Six flutes

Saxophone
Saxophone

Beautiful music
Belle musique

Beautiful dolls
Belle poupées

Cease Flute

Sock So Phone

Bell Moo Seek

Bell Poo Pay

Beautiful play
Belle pièce

Bell Pea Yes

Christmas
Noël

No Well

Beautiful statue
Belle statue

Bell Stott 2

Chairs *Les chaise*	**Lay Shay's**
Five beds *Cinq lits*	**Sank Lee**
Cables *Les fils*	**Lay Fee**
Videos *Des vidéos*	**Davey Day Oh**

Toilets *Les toilettes*	**Late Wall Let**
To the basement *Au sous-sol*	**Oh Sue Sole**
Beautiful photos *Les belles photos*	**Lay Bell Foe Toe**

SPORTS AND POLITICS

Skiing
Faire du ski

Fair Due Ski

Five cards
Cinq cartes

Sank Cart

Golf
Du golf

Due Golf

Hockey
Du hockey

Due Hoe Key

Tennis
Des tennis

Day 10 Knee

Politics
La politique

Lop Polly Teak

To the parade
Au défilé

Oh Day Fee Lay

It's a battle
C'est une bataille

Set Tune But Tie

Hills
Les collines

Lay Cole Lean

Nice air
Bel air

Bell Air

To the coast
À la cote

Allah Coat

To the lake
Au lac

Oh Lock

Some roses
Des roses

Day Rose

Beautiful tulips
Belles tulipes

Bell 2 Leap

Bouquet
Bouquet

Boo Kay

Birch trees
Des bouleaux

Day Boo Low

It's warm weather
Il fait chaud

Eel Fay Show

It's beautiful weather
Il fait beau

Eel Fay Bow

It's sunny out
Il y a du soleil

Eely Yacht Due So Lay

Is it nice weather?
Fait-il beau?

Fay Teal Bow?

How are you?
Comment t'allez-vous?

Comet Halley View?

That's dumb
C'est stupide

Say Stew Peed

That's foolish as a cabbage
C'est bête comme chou

Say Bet Come Shoe

That's baloney
C'est pisse d'âne

Say Peace Don

Who's farting?
Qui pète?

Key Pet?

Yeah
Ouais

Way

There isn't anything . . .
Il n'y en a pas . . .

Eel Knee Yawn a Pa . . .

I don't know
Je ne sais pas

Sh'Pa

I suppose
À la limite

Allah Lee Meat

Piece of cake
C'est du gateau

Say Due Got Toe

Appetizers
Hors d'oeuvre

Horse Ovaries

What will be will be
Que sera sera

Kay Said Ah Said Ah

You're cute
Tu es mignon

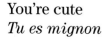

2A Mean Yawn

Ouch!
Aïe!

Eye

It's super
C'est super

Say Sue Pair

Oops
Oups

Oops